Eyewitness
DINOSAUR
Expert Files

Eyewitness
DINOSAUR
Expert Files

DK Publishing, Inc.

LONDON, NEW YORK,
MELBOURNE, MUNICH, AND DELHI

Consultant Professor Michael Benton
Senior Editor Jayne Miller
Project Editors Sarah Davis, Claire Ellerton
Senior Art Editors Joanne Little, David Ball
Art Editors Owen Peyton Jones, Peter Radcliffe,
Susan St.Louis, Gemma Thompson
Paper Engineer Alison Gardner
Managing Editor Camilla Hallinan
Art Director Martin Wilson
Publishing Manager Sunita Gahir
Category Publisher Andrea Pinnington
Picture Research Fran Vargo
DK Picture Library Rose Hossidge, Claire Bowers
Production Controller Angela Graef
DTP Designers Ronaldo Julien, Andy Hilliard
Jacket Designer Polly Appleton
Jacket Copywriter John Searcy

First published in the United States in 2007
by DK Publishing Limited,
375 Hudson Street, New York, New York 10014

07 08 09 10 11 10 9 8 7 6 5 4 3 2 1
ED509 – 07/07

A catalog record for this book is available
from the Library of Congress.

ISBN: 978–0–7566–3135–2

Color reproduction by Colourscan, Singapore
Printed and bound by Toppan Printing Co.
(Shenzhen) Ltd, China

Discover more at
www.dk.com

Contents

1

MEET THE EXPERTS

Ever wondered what it feels like to uncover historic fossil finds on a dig? Paleontologist Luis Chiappe relives one of his favorite and most famous trips, when he discovered an 80-million-year-old dinosaur nesting ground.

EXPERT

Paleontologist

PROFILE

NAME: **LUIS CHIAPPE**

NATIONALITY: **ARGENTINIAN**

LIVES: **US**

Dr Luis Chiappe has had a love of the outdoors since he was a child, prompted by regular weekend camping trips in the wild with his family. He is now the curator and director of the Dinosaur Institute at the Natural History Museum of Los Angeles County, which houses one of the largest fossil collections in the world. His main interest is researching the link between dinosaurs and their bird descendants. In 1997, he was on a dig in Patagonia in search of further clues to the connection between the two when he and fellow dinosaur experts Lowell Dingus and Rodolfo Coria discovered the largest collection of dinosaur nests and eggs in the world. Luis and his team of dedicated experts returned seven times over the following years to excavate further, patiently working through extreme heat, cold, and floods and living in difficult conditions to reveal a true treasure trove of finds. Luis has worked on and directed many dinosaur digs in Argentina, North America, and Central Asia over the years. Recently, he has helped to recover the skeleton of a *Tyrannosaurus rex* in Montana.

Valley of the Eggs

On a dig in a desolate area of Argentina, looking for something completely different, Luis Chiappe and his expedition team stumbled on an 80-million-year-old nesting site full of thousands of dinosaur eggs—and the first dinosaur babies to have been found with fossilized skin still on them.

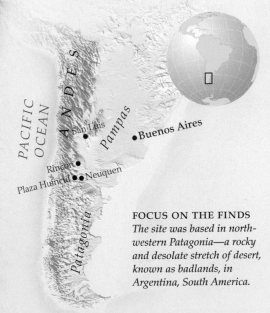

PACIFIC OCEAN

ANDES

Pampas

• San Luis

• Buenos Aires

Rincon •
Plaza Huincul • • Neuquen

Patagonia

FOCUS ON THE FINDS
The site was based in north-western Patagonia—a rocky and desolate stretch of desert, known as badlands, in Argentina, South America.

PREHISTORIC NEST
This rimmed dinosaur nest shows that the dinosaurs laid their clutch of eggs on the surface. The eggs, now sightly flattened, were once spherical and measured around 6 in (12 cm).

Historic discovery

When we went to Patagonia in November 1997 we were actually after something else! I had done a lot of research on early birds. Some fossils had been exposed and I had a feeling that other rocks farther north could yield more important finds that could point to the evolution of birds. We had chosen to explore Patagonia because it is one of the richest places on Earth to find dinosaurs and no one had ever been to this particular set of badlands before. We planned the trip and the team... and then we stumbled on the nesting site. This was so fascinating that we just had to switch our mission. In paleontology, as in all areas of science, you are frequently looking for something else when you make a discovery by chance.

A view of the quarry that produced about 500 eggs

Good timing

It was only the second day of our month-long field season. For a paleontology field trip, it was perfect. Often, the best discoveries are made on the last day of the season and you have to wait a year before returning to excavate further. It was also a relief to know that we would return home after the dig with something to show for the trip.

EGG HUNTING COUNTRY
Luis Chiappe and Lowell Dingus view the badlands. These are one of the world's finest dinosaur hunting grounds. The team found so many clutches they named the area Auca Mahuevo, after **mas huevos,** *Spanish for "more eggs."*

Excavating eggs in the quarry at Auca Mahuevo

> *"Wow! I can't even begin to describe the feeling— and the importance of the find. I get goosebumps just thinking about it"*

DINOSAUR SKIN
A patch of fossilized skin shows the details that covered the body of the baby dinosaurs. The find revealed for the first time how the babies' skin looked.

Strip of larger scales

Eggs underfoot

I have worked in many incredible sites, but there is nothing like that place. You are walking on eggs everywhere you go, there's such a wealth of finds. We made our discoveries just by prospecting— walking and looking at the ground. We saw a tip of something exposed, and then started to excavate, to brush away the soil around it. We found dozens of egg clutches all over the site. Then we started to look for embryos, the unborn baby dinosaurs. They would be a clue to whose nests we had found.

Unhatched baby dinosaurs

A few days after we found the egg clusters we started to find bits of bones inside the eggs, and then traces of the babies' skin. There has been no other instance of finding skin on an unhatched dinosaur. It was an absolute first. There's a funny story about it, though. One of my team members came up with a piece of egg with a bumpy surface, wondering if it could be the skin of a baby. I said that sounded highly unlikely. A few days passed by, then I found a very big chunk of skin—it was undoubtedly skin. It seemed as if I admitted it was skin because I had found it! That's not the case, of course! Our digs are team efforts, and everyone makes a contribution, so I feel happy for the results of the team over and above personal discoveries. Even so, everyone likes to find something special!

Some questions

We found more than 100 specimens of fossilized dinosaur babies. I can't begin to describe the feeling—and the importance of the find. You had to be there to believe it. I get goosebumps just thinking about it. The discoveries raised many questions. The biggest one was: whose eggs were they? And what kind of catastrophe caused such devastation that it resulted in the burial of an entire nesting colony, with so many thousands of eggs? Why were there so many eggs in one place?

MOLDING
Technician Adrian Garrido pours silicon rubber over a clutch of eggs to create a mold of an entire nest. This will later be used to reconstruct a nest.

MAPPING
Egg expert Frankie Jackson uses a grid of strings, which divides an area into small sections, to map the location of the eggs within a clutch.

Teamwork

Dinosaur hunting teams are usually between 15 and 25 people. The team depends on the situation. Ours was a big team. We had 25–30 people, but that could change. Imagine, we are away for five weeks, some people can spare only two weeks, others are local people helping during vacations or for a couple of days. We had an influx of local students. This area is remote, but not that inaccessible—people can get to us.

Grilled armadillos from Omar the chef

Osvaldo Di Iorio eyes a tarantula

Camp life

When I have a team of 20–25 people to cater for, it's far easier to hire a cook and a camp manager, so I don't have to worry. Someone who stays in the camp, who has cooked food ready for us, takes care of the dishes, tells me when we're running out of eggs or milk, and can go into town to buy apples. Someone essentially to look after the practical side. It is hard enough to camp for five-week stretches sometimes, so these things make it bearable. It's not like conquering Everest, but there's a lot of roughing it. There are no bathrooms or running water—you use whatever bush is around and can't take regular showers! All kinds of animals are around and creatures that crawl in your sleeping bag! Some elements were hard to bear—getting washed away by storms, shivering in the cold, and rains often result in the appearance of these enormous spiders that crawl over every surface! There was a real risk

of getting lost in the badlands or being stranded because of flash floods, but we were able to get out and could get emergency rescue if needed. Luckily, we had no serious problems.

Experts on call

We were a mixed team of experts and researchers from different disciplines, or areas of interest. Paleontologists essentially look at fossils but some may come with an expertise on meat-eating dinosaurs or plant-eating dinosaurs. An expert on eggshells could help prove that the eggs belonged to dinosaurs and not birds. We had an entomologist, Osvaldo Di Iorio, who studied insects, and geologists to look at ancient layers of soil and tell us how old the rocks were. I'd put together a team beforehand, but once the eggs were discovered we invited others, including two Ph.D. students who were doing studies on dinosaur eggs and were obviously knowledgable on the subject.

Media and tourists

We also had a lot of visitors to the site who weren't connected with the team—media and tourists! We had an enormous amount of media attention and there were camera crews and reporters around. Then, as news of the discovery got out, we started getting people who were curious to see the site. Hundreds of them. We were only 3–4 hours away from a city of almost 300,000 people. It's always going to happen. It turns into a Sunday picnic! Aside from the accidental damage and disruption caused by so many interested people, there is deliberate looting and vandalism and breaking of eggs. In this particular case there was a money side too—we have found pieces of looted dinosaur eggs on eBay selling for 15 dollars! Yet every piece of eggshell is priceless to scientists.

Finding a dinosaur

Aside from the eggs, we discovered a horned meat-eating dinosaur buried in what had once been a lake. The bones were lying together and included the feet, which had never been found before for this kind of meat-eating dinosaur. We knew that if there were so many eggs being laid then there must

EXCAVATING EGGS
Eggs are slowly uncovered by a crew of paleontologists. In an area roughly 200–300 yd (185–275 m), the crew found about 195 clusters of eggs, each with 6–12 eggs. Some were taken away for analysis, but hundreds were left at the site.

have been something killing the babies—a reason for even more eggs being laid. Now we had found a likely reason. The dinosaur we uncovered was *Aucasaurus*, a predator, which we think may have attacked in packs, picking out the baby dinosaurs as they hatched. There had been meat-eaters living in the midst of the mothers and their babies.

Detective work

We had guessed that the eggs belonged to sauropods, because their shape and size were similar to others that had been found elsewhere. Sauropods are huge, plant-eating dinosaurs with long necks. Over the five-week excavation, we collected about 80 embryo fossils, a large number of eggs, and information about how these dinosaurs lived and nested. We also collected evidence of the age of these dinosaurs—all of which we could take back to the lab for research to find some more answers.

COLLECTING AUCASAURUS
Dinosaur expert Rodolfo Coria and other team members create a plaster jacket over the bones of the meat-eating Aucasaurus, *a 20 ft-(6 m-) long menace for the long-necked, plant-eating sauropods who laid their eggs.*

PULLING THE JACKET
The Auca Mahuevo team hauls a heavy plaster jacket containing an intact clutch of eggs—these eggs were taken to a museum in Patagonia.

"Because of these finds, we have a far better snapshot of dinosaurs from 80 million years ago"

Owning a dinosaur

There are laws over fossil finds that all international expeditions have to follow. Although the dig was organized for the National History Museum of Los Angeles County, we were working in Argentina— the fossils belong there. Many of the finds went to the Carmen Funes Museum of Patagonia, and scientists and students at Argentinian colleges will have access to them. We were allowed to take some eggs away for research, and we mounted an exhibition at the NHM in LA, but the finds all had to be sent back. The important thing isn't owning the fossils—we're happy to have been able to do some research, that's how it works. We do have millions of photos of all the finds!

It's a wrap

After that first expedition in November 1997, we had a whole bunch of fossils that needed to be prepared to transport them safely to the museum. The clutches and embryos we collected had to be wrapped in protective layers. To stop them from crumbling or shattering, we use toilet paper, plaster, and burlap sacking to create a "jacket". Each specimen is given a field number. This is written on the jacket, along with any special instructions to help the preparator back in the lab where they will be carefully cleaned and examined under microscopes.

DETAILED WORK
Dinosaur Institute's lab manager Doug Goodreau prepares a clutch of eggs at the Natural History Museum of Los Angeles County. Detailed reasearch is performed in the museum lab.

A window on their world

The egg clutches were still encased in surrounding rock, or matrix, which had to be scraped away to reveal the fossils. We went for the traditional approach and opened

Sergio Saldivia, Carmen Funes Museum

Preparing the Auca Mahuevo eggs

a flood, muddy water covered the nests, and the eggs lying in the mud were suffocated. The site was buried.

Follow-up work

We found all this out by revisiting the site over the years to answer further questions. We're eager to dispel the myth of that Indiana Jones-style of fossil hunting—collecting something and then thinking, what's next? This is paleontology. Our project is more careful. We returned seven times to continue excavation and data gathering, and in between we did research. We have written 20–25 papers (and a book) on that site, and there are years of research left. I love the research and I love the writing. I really love my work!

windows in the shells to expose an embryo. There were so many eggs that at the expense of a few we could cut some so they could be studied. We found the eggs were laid by titanosaurs, and without embryos we couldn't have done that. The pattern of bumps on the skin of our Patagonian babies is remarkably similar to the pattern of armor plating in the skin of *Saltasaurus*, a titanosaur found in Argentina.

A clearer picture

Discovering the egg site led to more information about the dinosaurs, the babies, and the area. Because of these finds we have a much better snapshot of dinosaurs from around 80 million years ago. We can picture a large group of mothers scooping sand and laying eggs there, leaving eggs to incubate (develop) in the sun, and of babies hatching in huge numbers.

Mass destruction

So what went wrong? The nests were on a flood plain hundreds of feet away from a river. There was

shell

baby dinosaur bones

ANCIENT EGG
The tiny bones of an unhatched baby dinosaur poke beneath the shell of this grapefruit-sized egg. Another opened egg revealed bones of an embryo skull, and under a microscope, tiny teeth about ⅛ in (2 mm) long.

TITANOSAURS
Experts believe the eggs belonged to sauropod dinosaurs called titanosaurs, once common in South America. Fossils of these animals were found in rocks near the eggs.

Types of Expert

MANY DIFFERENT TYPES of knowledge and skill are needed to help us discover and understand what dinosaurs were like and how they lived. From the scientists who know where to find the fossils to the artists who create the life-like models, a wealth of expertise is required.

RE-CREATING ENVIRONMENTS
This Edmontonia *model is part of an exhibition at the Royal Tyrrell Museum of Paleontology in Alberta, Canada. An important part of the exhibit is its background, which has been created to look like a Cretaceous woodland environment, based on fossil evidence of plants from that time.*

GEOLOGIST

A geologist studies the physical structure and processes of the Earth. One aspect of this research involves examining rocks and how they are formed. This can help scientists to understand what the Earth was like millions of years ago, including what kinds of life existed then and in what kind of environment. Fossils preserved in rock layers provide information about specific forms of prehistoric life, including fossilized plants and leaves that can provide clues as to the climate and vegetation at that time.

ROCK LAYERS
A geologist examines fossils exposed on the rock surface near Lyell Icefield, in the Canadian Rocky Mountains. Fossils buried deep in the rock layers have been laid bare by water and weather gradually eroding the rock.

FOSSIL COLLECTOR

There are a number of different types of fossil collector. Scientists collect fossils as an important part of their research work. Some people hunt for fossils as a hobby. Others are more commercially minded, searching for fossils that they can then sell to shops or museums. College students may help on digs during their vacations. Tasks might involve mapping bones or helping to free fossils from their surrounding rock, and wrapping them in plaster to protect them.

STUDENTS ON A DIG
A couple of students are mapping the position of some dinosaur bones embedded in the rock surface at a site in Aude sur la Campagne, Languedoc-Roussillon, France.

FOSSIL
This fossil of a curved hand claw was found in Britain along with other remains of a large meat-eating dinosaur. It may have used its claw to catch fish to eat.

PALEONTOLOGIST

A paleontologist studies ancient life by looking at plant and animal fossils. Initially, he or she undertakes careful research to find out where fossil-rich sedimentary rock occurs. Sometimes large teams of paleontologists go on expeditions to find and excavate dinosaur fossils. Once on site, their first job is to record the exact positions of any bones they discover. Next they use suitable tools to extract them. The bones may need to be covered in plaster jackets to prevent them from getting damaged during removal from the site. The fossils are then transported to a laboratory for detailed study.

EXCAVATION
A paleontologist oversees the unearthing of a theropod bone. The position in which it is found, and the direction in which it is pointing, are key pieces of information in rebuilding the picture of how the animal looked.

OVERSEEING THE DIG
Paleontologist Phil Currie, in a purple shirt, oversees a dig along the Red Deer River, in Canada. The site is in an area containing one of the most famous fossil beds in the world. The remains of around 40 dinosaur species from the Cretaceous period have been found there, including **Tyrannosaurus rex.**

CURATOR

It is a curator's job to look after museum artifacts and exhibits. When a dinosaur skeleton arrives in the museum, the curator oversees the unpacking and cleaning of the bones, and plans what to do with them—will they go into storage, so they can be studied by paleontologists from around the world, or should they go on exhibit? There isn't room to put everything on display, but people love to see something new. Planning and fund-raising for new exhibits can take years. Curators also follow up research requests from the public, and develop education programs for visitors and the local community.

ASSEMBLING THE EXHIBIT

Workers in a hydraulic crane weld together the frame of a model Barosaurus at the American Museum of Natural History. Only copies of original bones are used in exhibits. The original bones would be too fragile, and are usually stored away for further study.

ARTIST'S IMPRESSION
A conservator in the paleontology department at the Natural History Museum in London, England, cleans up a fossil of a feathered **Dromaeosaurus,** *whare is nicknamed "Fuzzy Raptor."*

ARTIST

Dinosaur artists often work closely with paleontologists in order to create vivid reconstructions of prehistoric creatures. They may also spend years of independent research studying dinosaurs and the environment in which they lived. Today, dinosaur art can be created using digital technology. A dinosaur's skeleton is measured, and the measurements are used to create a grid that plots the shape of the dinosaur in three dimensions.

MODEL MAKERS
A museum technician paints a model of **Scipionyx,** *a small, fast theropod known only from a single hatchling. The artist uses his imagination when coloring the model.*

PREPARATORS

Fossil preparators work closely with paleontologists to prepare fossils for scientific analysis. This involves removing the fossils from their surrounding rock, or matrix, and cleaning them. Saws and drills are used to cut away large chunks of rock. Vibrating handheld tools, called scribe tools, remove smaller pieces of rock close to the actual fossil. Lasers can also be used to burn surface pollutants off fossil bones. Once cleaned, the bones may be treated with chemicals to conserve them.

DINOSAUR LAB
Museum workers clean the fossilized remains of dinosaur bones in the laboratory at the Royal Tyrrell Museum, Canada. It is a painstaking and highly skilled process that may take years to complete.

Reconstruction

A RECONSTRUCTED SKELETON provides the framework for scientists to build a model of a dinosaur as it might have looked in real life. It is often necessary to guess the shape and size of any missing bones. Marks on the bones where muscles were once attached can give clues about the size and shape of the body that once fleshed out the bones. Other fossil evidence may provide information about the dinosaur's skin and how it moved.

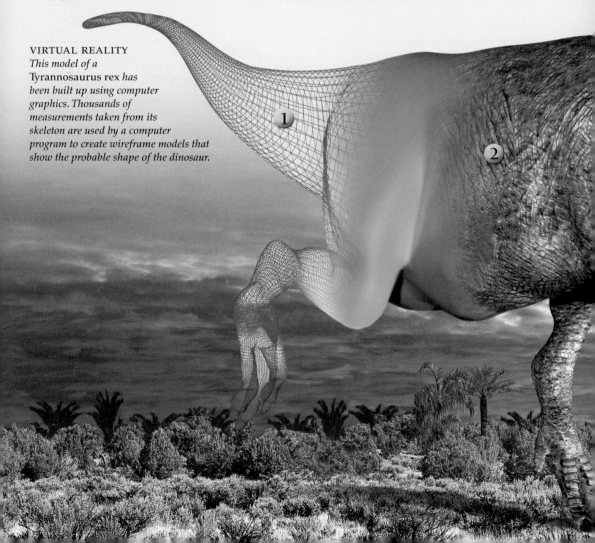

VIRTUAL REALITY
This model of a
Tyrannosaurus rex *has*
been built up using computer
graphics. Thousands of
measurements taken from its
skeleton are used by a computer
program to create wireframe models that
show the probable shape of the dinosaur.

GOING ON SHOW
Technicians assemble a replica Allosaurus *skeleton as part of the spectacular display at the American Museum of Natural History.*

MAKING MODELS
A reconstructed skeleton is usually made using lightweight casts of fossil bones. This modeler is filling casts with liquid foam plastic.

1. *Surface mesh:* Tyrannosaurus's *body shape is created using a computer-generated 3-D grid*

2. *Texture: skin texture is added to the mesh, based on fossil evidence and comparisons with similar living animals*

3. *Movement: stretches and wrinkles are added to the skin to help show how the dinosaur moved its body*

4. *Color: realistic color tones are based on those of modern animals with a similar lifestyle to the dinosaur*

Hall of Fame

ALL OF THE PEOPLE on these pages have made an important contribution to our knowledge of the history of dinosaurs, from finding the first bones of a new species to developing theories about how these prehistoric creatures evolved and lived.

MARY ANNING

1799–1847

JOB: Fossil Collector

COUNTRY: UK

Mary Anning was born in Lyme Regis, England, an area rich in fossils. Following in her father's footsteps, Mary Anning became a pioneering fossil collector and key figure in early paleontology. In 1811, she discovered the fossil skeleton of a Jurassic ichthyosaur, which is now in London's Natural History Museum. She went on to discover the first plesiosaur in 1821 and the first pterodactyl in 1828. Most of the fossils collected by Anning were sold to institutions and private collections, but often no record was kept of her role in the discovery.

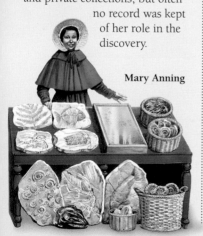

Mary Anning

ROBERT BAKKER

1945–PRESENT

JOB: Paleontologist

COUNTRY: US

Robert Bakker has been largely credited with reshaping modern theory about dinosaurs. He is best known for his revolutionary idea that dinosaurs are hot-blooded relatives of birds rather than cold-blooded giant lizards. Immense enthusiasm for his subject matter led not only to his becoming an advisor on the film *The Lost World: Jurassic Park* (1997), but also to the bearded paleontologist character, Dr. Robert Burke, being modeled on Bakker.

Robert Bakker

RINCHEN BARSBOLD

1935–PRESENT

JOB: Paleontologist

COUNTRY: Mongolia

Rinchen Barsbold has been key in the discovery and recovery of one of the largest dinosaur collections in the world. His work has projected Mongolian paleontology into world prominence. Director of the Institute of Geology at the Mongolian Academy of Sciences, Barsbold discovered many new dinosaurs, naming *Adasaurus* and *Enigmosauridae* in 1983, *Conchoraptor* in 1985, *Anserimimus* in 1988, and *Nomingia* in 2000. *Barsboldia*, a 30 ft- (10 m-) long, duck-billed dinosaur, which lived in Mongolia in the Late Cretaceous, was named after Barsbold in 1981.

JOSE BONAPARTE

1928–PRESENT

JOB: Paleontologist

COUNTRY: Argentina

Born in Rosario, Argentina, and affiliated with the Argentine Museum of Natural Sciences, Bonaparte is responsible for mentoring a new generation of Argentine paleontologists. He discovered a wealth of South American dinosaurs and carried out outstanding work on the theropods he found there.

BARNUM BROWN

1879–1968

JOB: Fossil Hunter

COUNTRY: US

Barnum Brown is credited as the greatest dinosaur hunter of the 20th century. He excavated the first documented remains of *Tyrannosaurus rex* in 1902. Brown went on to recover a variety of complex dinosaur skeletons from the Red Deer River in Alberta,

Canada. One of Brown's most significant finds, made in 1910, were several hind feet from a group of *Albertosaurus* collected in Dry Island Provincial Park. In the 1930s, Brown excavated a wealth of Jurassic fossils at Howe Ranch, Wyoming. As a representative of the American Museum of Natural History, he also acquired fossils from all over the world.

WILLIAM BUCKLAND
1784–1856
JOB: Clergyman/Geologist
COUNTRY: UK

As a boy growing up in Devon, England, William Buckland used to go on walks with his father where he would collect fossils from Jurassic rocks exposed in quarries. His interest in geology continued and in 1813, having completed studies for the ministry and been ordained as a clergyman, he was appointed reader of mineralogy at Corpus Christi College, Oxford. In 1824, after becoming president of the Geological Society, London, he announced the discovery of fossil bones of a giant reptile, which he named *Megalosaurus* ("great lizard"). He wrote what was to become the first detailed account of a dinosaur.

EDWARD DRINKER COPE
1840–1897
JOB: Paleontologist
COUNTRY: US

Edward Drinker Cope—professor of natural science at Haverford College, and then professor of geology and paleontology at the University of Pennsylvania— specialized in the

study of the American fossil vertebrates. From 1871 to 1877 he carried out geological explorations in Kansas, Wyoming, and Colorado. He made known at least 1,000 new species. Among these were 56 species of dinosaur, including *Camarasaurus* and *Coelophysis*. He was also a prolific publisher, producing more than 1,200 scientific papers in his lifetime.

GEORGES CUVIER
1769–1832
JOB: Naturalist
COUNTRY: France

Georges Cuvier was one of the most influential figures in science during the early 19th century. His work is considered the foundation of vertebrate paleontology and it was said that he could reconstruct a skeleton based on a single bone. Cuvier convinced his contemporaries that extinction of past life forms was a fact—it had been a controversial speculation before.

Zhiming Dong

ZHIMING DONG
1937–PRESENT
JOB: Paleontologist
COUNTRY: China

Dong has become China's most famous paleontologist, and has led fossil-finding expeditions to the Gobi Desert, Mongolia, and China's Yunnan province. His most important discovery was at Dashanpu quarry in Sichuan Province, China, where in 1979 he found skeletons of more than 100 dinosaurs, most of them sauropods, including five rare sauropod skulls.

Charles W. Gilmore

CHARLES W. GILMORE
1874–1945
JOB: Paleontologist
COUNTRY: US

Gilmore studied North American and Asian dinosaurs and worked extensively in the Gobi Desert. He named several dinosaur species, including *Bactrosaurus,* a Late Cretaceous duck-billed ornithopod with a flat head and long spines running along its back, and *Alamosaurus*, the last known sauropod and North America's only known titanosaur. The dinosaur *Gilmoreosaurus*, found in China in 1979 was named in his honor. Gilmore devoted much time to the study of Jurassic sauropods.

EDWARD B. HITCHCOCK
1793–1864

JOB: Clergyman/Geologist

COUNTRY: US

Edward B. Hitchcock was president and professor of Natural Theology and Geology at Amherst College, New England. He collected and described more than 20,000 fossil footprints from Triassic rocks of Connecticut, without knowing that they were dinosaur tracks. To his dying day, Hitchcock believed that he had unearthed the tracks of ancient birds.

FRIEDRICH VON HUENE
1875–1969

JOB: Paleontologist

COUNTRY: Germany

Friedrich von Huene named more dinosaurs in the early 20th century than anyone else in Europe. His discoveries include the skeletons of a herd of more than 35 *Plateosaurus*, found buried in a mudslide, the early proto-dinosaur *Saltopus*, which was a sharp-toothed carnivore about the size of a cat, the giant South American sauropod *Antarctosaurus*, and many other dinosaurs and animals such as pterosaurs.

THOMAS H. HUXLEY
1825–1895

JOB: Scientist

COUNTRY: UK

Thomas Huxley studied medicine at Charing Cross Hospital. He subsequently went on a naval voyage as assistant surgeon and conducted scientific research on marine life. A friend of the famous evolutionary theorist Charles Darwin, Huxley was the first scientist to notice the similarity between birds and dinosaurs. His study of fossil reptiles led to his demonstrating, at a lecture he gave at the Royal College of Surgeons in 1867, the basic similarity between the two groups, which he united under the title of Sauropsida.

LAWRENCE MORRIS LAMBE
1849–1934

JOB: Geologist/Paleontologist

COUNTRY: Canada

Lawrence Morris Lambe worked for the Canadian Geographical Survey and hunted for fossils near Alberta, Canada. His published writings on the many interesting dinosaur finds he made helped bring dinosaurs into the public eye. As a result, dinosaur hunters from all over the world descended on Alberta. Lambe discovered a number of new dinosaurs. *Lambeosaurus*, a hadrosaur, was named after him in 1923.

Othniel Marsh

GIDEON MANTELL
1790–1852

JOB: Amateur Fossil Hunter

COUNTRY: UK

Gideon Mantell was one of the very first fossil hunters. In 1822, while out walking in the English countryside with his wife, he (or possibly she) came across a very large tooth embedded in a rock. He could tell that it belonged to a plant-eater, but only identified it as a reptile three years later. Because of its similarity to an iguana, he decided to call it *Iguanodon*, and published his description in 1825. It was the second dinosaur ever to be named.

OTHNIEL MARSH
1831–1899

JOB: Paleontologist

COUNTRY: US

A paleontologist from Yale University, Othniel Marsh named roughly 500 new species of fossil animals, all discovered by himself and his team of fossil hunters. During the 1870s, Marsh led his students on four fossil-hunting expeditions to western North America. A

Sir Richard Owen

turning point on one of these expeditions was the discovery of a bird's skull with teeth in its beak, which seemed to prove that birds have evolved from reptiles. This backed up Charles Darwin's theory that animals evolve over time into new species. In this case, the evidence suggested that certain types of dinosaur evolved into birds.

SIR RICHARD OWEN
1804–1892

JOB: Anatomist

COUNTRY: UK

In 1842, Sir Richard Owen coined the term Dinosauria (from the Greek *deinos* meaning "terrible," and *sauros* meaning "lizard"), having identified the creatures as a suborder of large, extinct reptiles. Owen also named and described many dinosaurs, among them *Cetiosaurus*, *Echinodon*, *Massospondylus*, and *Scelidosaurus*. He worked closely with sculptor Benjamin Waterhouse Hawkins on the construction of life-size dinosaur models for the Crystal Palace exhibition in London.

HARRY GOVIER SEELEY
1839–1909
JOB: Paleontologist
COUNTRY: UK

While a student at Cambridge University, Harry Govier Seeley became assistant to Adam Sedgwick, one of the great founders of geology. He was later offered a position at the British Museum, but turned it down to pursue his own work. Seeley's most important contribution was to establish that dinosaurs fell into two main groups, the saurischians and the ornithischians, based on the structure of their pelvic bones. He also described and named numerous dinosaurs from their fossils, among them *Craterosaurus* and *Agrosaurus*.

PAUL SERENO
1958–PRESENT
JOB: Paleontologist
COUNTRY: US

Paul Sereno studied art and biology before becoming a paleontologist at the University of Chicago in 1987. He has discovered dinosaurs in five continents and led many expeditions. He took his first field trip in 1988, to the Andes foothills in Argentina. There he and his team unearthed fossils of two of the earliest dinosaurs, *Herrerasaurus* and *Eoraptor*. In 1990 Sereno led expeditions into Niger and Morocco, where he found some new and unusual dinosaurs such as *Afrovenator*, a 27 ft- (8.2 m-) long carnivore, *Jobaria*, a 70 ft- (21.3 m-) long herbivore, and *Suchomimus*, a fish-eating dinosaur with a sail on its back. Sereno has also taken expeditions into India and the Gobi Desert, Mongolia.

Paul Sereno

XING XU
DATES
JOB: Paleontologist
COUNTRY: China

A member of the Chinese Institute of Vertebrate Paleontology and Paleoanthropology in Beijing, Xing Xu is famous for having named numerous dinosaurs, including the Jurassic dinosaur *Yinlong*. The *Yinlong* discovery consisted of a single beautifully preserved skeleton, complete with skull, found in 2004 in China's Xinjiang Province. Another dinosaur, *Guanlong*, a feathered relative of *Tyrannosaurus rex*, was named by Xing Xu in 2006.

Chung Chien Young

CHUNG CHIEN YOUNG
DATES 1897–1979
JOB: Paleontologist
COUNTRY: China

Also known as Yang Zhongijan, the so-called "Father of Chinese vertebrate paleontology" was one of China's most important fossil scientists. He brought international attention to Chinese dinosaurs and inspired the current generation of paleontologists. Young oversaw the collection and study of Chinese dinosaurs fom 1933 through to the 1970s. Among the most important of these were the prosauropods, *Lufengosaurus* and *Yunnanosaurus*, the immense sauropod *Mamenchisaurus*, and China's first stegosaur.

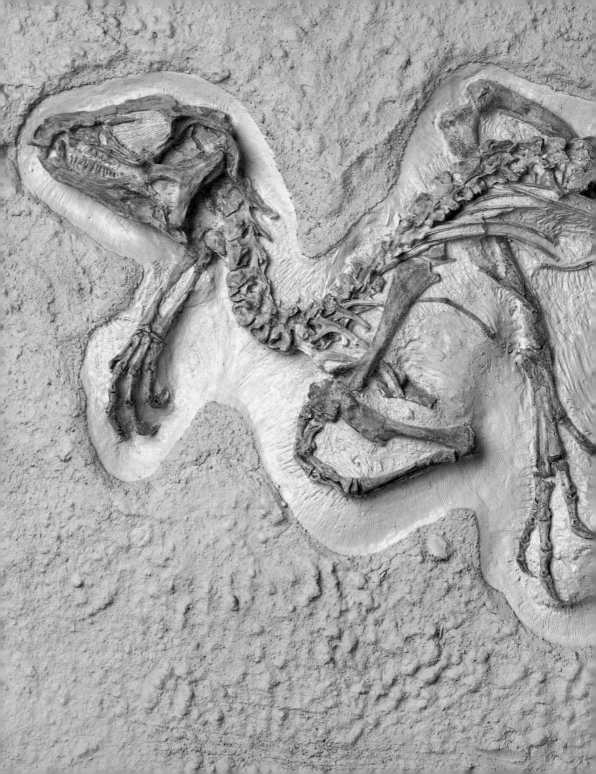

2

ACTIVITIES

Have you got what it takes to be a paleontologist? Find out how much you know and hone your skills with our challenging activities.

Which expert are you?

Inspired by the experts in your pack, you've decided you'd like to work with dinosaurs. But there are so many fascinating areas to go into—which will you choose? Use this fun flowchart to help you out!

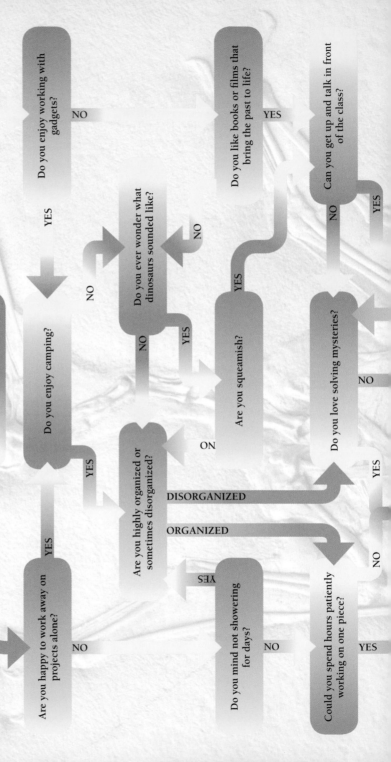

START HERE

Where would you most like to work—in a city office or outdoors?

CITY OFFICE

OUTDOORS

Do you enjoy camping?

YES

NO

Do you enjoy working with gadgets?

NO

YES

Are you highly organized or sometimes disorganized?

DISORGANIZED

ORGANIZED

Do you ever wonder what dinosaurs sounded like?

NO

YES

NO

Are you squeamish?

YES

NO

Do you like books or films that bring the past to life?

YES

Can you get up and talk in front of the class?

NO

YES

Do you love solving mysteries?

YES

NO

Are you happy to work away on projects alone?

YES

NO

Do you mind not showering for days?

YES

NO

Could you spend hours patiently working on one piece?

NO

YES

ON

Do you like to see treasures restored?

YES

Would you enjoy working around noisy, excitable children?

YES

NO

Are you interested in the anatomy of animals?

YES

Do you like model making?

YES

NO

Would you examine dino poop?

NO

YES

NO

Do you see dinosaur skeletons where others see rocks?

YES

NO

Are you good at jigsaw puzzles?

NO

YES

PALEONTOLOGIST

You enjoy working outdoors in a team and are naturally organized. You are patient yet inquisitive and willing to rough it to fulfill your dream of uncovering a dino!

LAB TECHNICIAN

You are good at analyzing, researching, and collating data. You are happy working with high-tech gadgets and love solving mysteries.

BIOLOGIST

You are intrigued by animals, how they survive, and how their bodies function. You are happy getting your hands dirty and enjoy practical work, even the gory stuff!

CURATOR

You like historic artefacts. You have a creative eye, and a knack for knowing how to get the public enthusiastic about the past and helping experts with their research.

Living cousins

Some of today's animals share features with prehistoric animals that are now extinct. Each description in the box is a shared characteristic between a dinosaur and a living animal. Draw a line between the related animals then write their shared feature along the line. See if you can complete each dinosaur name, too.

SHARED FEATURES
Horned face
Armor-plated skin
Fast runner
Wide, flat beak
Flesh-ripping teeth
Long neck

Armadillo

Duck-billed platypus

S _ I _ M _ _ _ S

🔍 Find me among lots of food in *Eyewitness Dinosaur*.

_ L _ _ S _ _ R _ S

🔍 I'm a big meat-eater. Check out my teeth in *Eyewitness Dinosaur*.

Giraffe

Ostrich

Lion

Rhinoceros

T _ _ C _ _ T _ P _
Look in *Eyewitness Dinosaur* for my three-horned face.

C _ _ Y T _ _ _ A _ R _ S
I'm also known as a hadrosaur in *Eyewitness Dinosaur*.

G _ LL _ _ _ M _ S
Built for speed, you'll see me charging around *Eyewitness Dinosaur*.

_ D M _ _ _ O _ _ A
I'm thick-skinned according to *Eyewitness Dinosaur*.

Who am I?

More than 700 species of dinosaur have been named, all unique in size, shape, diet, and habits. But can you tell them apart? Identify these dinosaurs and find out the meaning of their names, then circle the type of food they eat.

Use the Profile Cards to help you out.

1. Name

....
Meaning

....
MEAT / PLANTS / BOTH

2. Name

....
Meaning

....
MEAT / PLANTS / BOTH

3. Name

....
Meaning

....
MEAT / PLANTS / BOTH

4. Name

....
Meaning

....
MEAT / PLANTS / BOTH

6. Name

....

Meaning

....

MEAT / PLANTS / BOTH

7. Name

....

Meaning

....

MEAT / PLANTS / BOTH

5. Name

....

Meaning

....

MEAT / PLANTS / BOTH

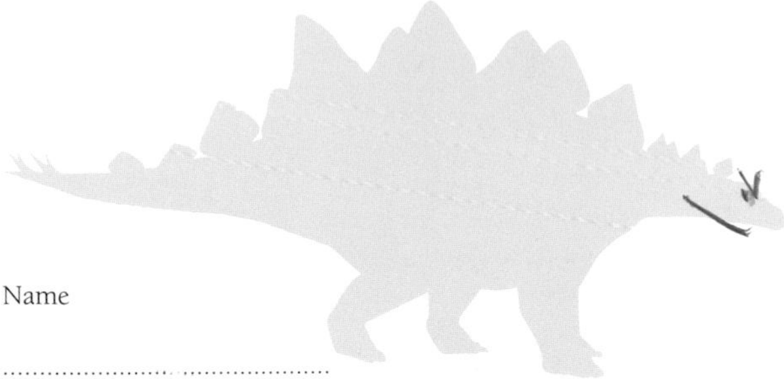

8. Name

....

Meaning

....

MEAT / PLANTS / BOTH

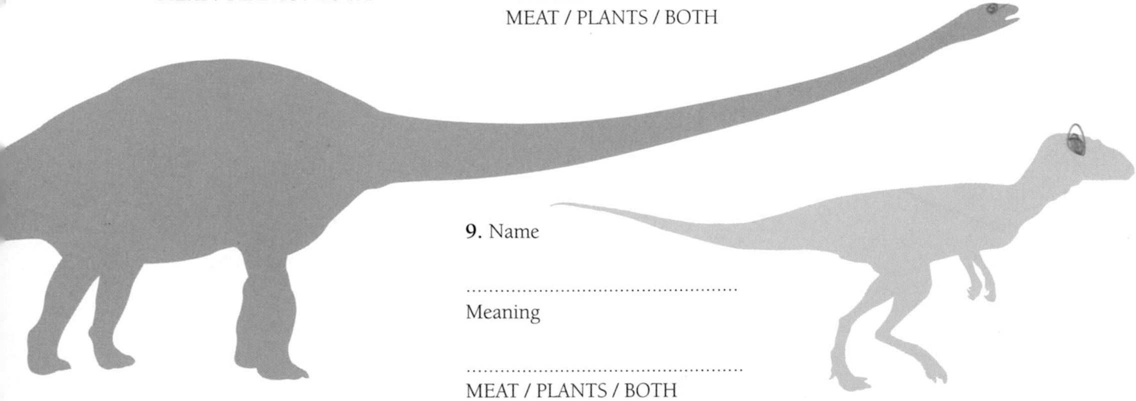

9. Name

....

Meaning

....

MEAT / PLANTS / BOTH

10. Name

....

Meaning

....

MEAT / PLANTS / BOTH

HOW LONG
DID IT TAKE YOU?

☐ 10 mins:
Expert

☐ 15 mins:
Knowledgable

☐ 20 mins:
Beginner

Dino diets

Experts learn a lot from teeth—most importantly, what food dinosaurs ate. Circle the correct diets for these prehistoric animals. You'll find the answers in *Eyewitness Dinosaur*, but can you spot the odd-dinosaur-out?

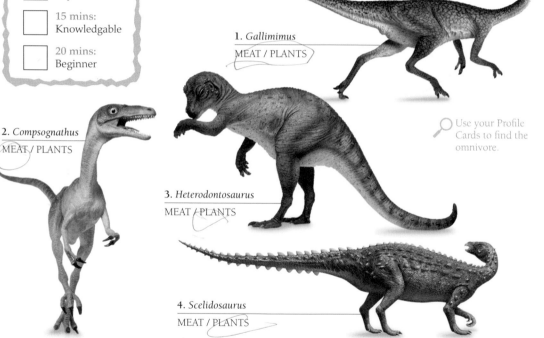

1. *Gallimimus*
MEAT / PLANTS

2. *Compsognathus*
MEAT / PLANTS

○ Use your Profile
Cards to find the
omnivore.

3. *Heterodontosaurus*
MEAT / PLANTS

4. *Scelidosaurus*
MEAT / PLANTS

Botanical quiz

Can you spot
any food that
wouldn't have
been around in
dinosaur times?

Liverwort

Conifer

Cabbage

Fern

5. *Hypsilophodon*
MEAT / PLANTS

6. *Parasaurolophus*
MEAT / PLANTS

7. *Coelophysis*
MEAT / PLANTS

8. *Deinonychus*
MEAT / PLANTS

9. *Iguanodon*
MEAT / PLANTS

If you like your "greens"
you won't go hungry in
Eyewitness Dinosaur.

Horsetail

Cycad

Magnolia

Wheat

Name game

A dinosaur's name often hints at what it looked like, who it was related to, who found it, or where it was found. Look at the lists of names and meanings and see if you can link them to the right dinosaurs.

Use the Profile Cards for extra help.

LEVEL 2

How long did it take you?

☐ 10 mins: Expert

☐ 15 mins: Knowledgable

☐ 20 mins: Beginner

1. Name

....

Meaning

....

2. Name

....

Meaning

....

3. Name

....

Meaning

....

NAMES
─────────
Herrerasaurus
Oviraptor
Protoceratops
Psittacosaurus
Tyrannosaurus rex
Maiasaura

MEANING
─────────
"Good mother lizard"
"Egg thief"
"First-horned face"
"Herrera's lizard"
"King of the tyrant lizards"
"Parrot lizard"

4. Name

....

Meaning

....

5. Name

....

Meaning

....

6. Name

....

Meaning

....

Mixed up

Can you unscramble the letters to make dinosaur names?

1. RATORVELOCIP

....

2. OPHYSCELOSI

....

3. GNUNOODIA

....

4. MUMSAGILIL

....

5. OSAURSCELIDUS

....

6. SUCODIPLOD

....

7. TORNUURSASOB

....

8. YAXONBRY

....

Which of the above dinosaurs has been renamed *Apatosaurus*?

....

Play Hide and Seek in *Eyewitness Dinosaur* to find these answers.

Label it

Experts assembling a skeleton like this need to know a great deal about anatomy. They have to identify fragments from tiny teeth to giant femurs, work out which family the dinosaur belonged to, and piece it together like a jigsaw puzzle. Test your knowledge by seeing how many bones you can label.

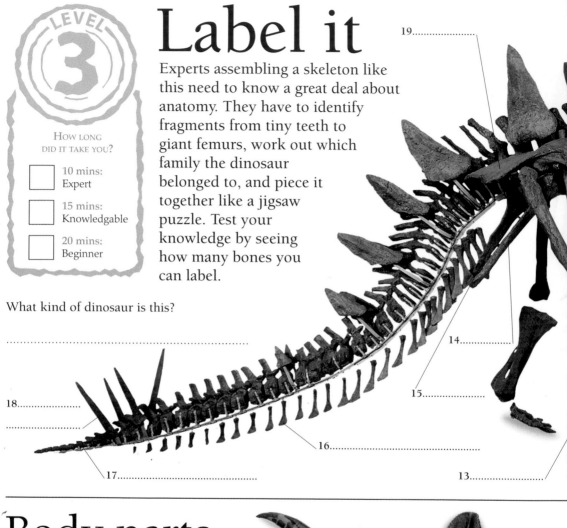

19..........

14..................

15....................

18....................
....

16..

17...

13...........................

What kind of dinosaur is this?

....

Body parts

Most of the information we have about dinosaurs comes from fossilized remains like these. Can you name the body parts and then find out which dinosaurs they came from?

A.

B.

🔍 Dig up the evidence from *Eyewitness Dinosaur.*

Dinosaur

....

Dinosaur

....

....

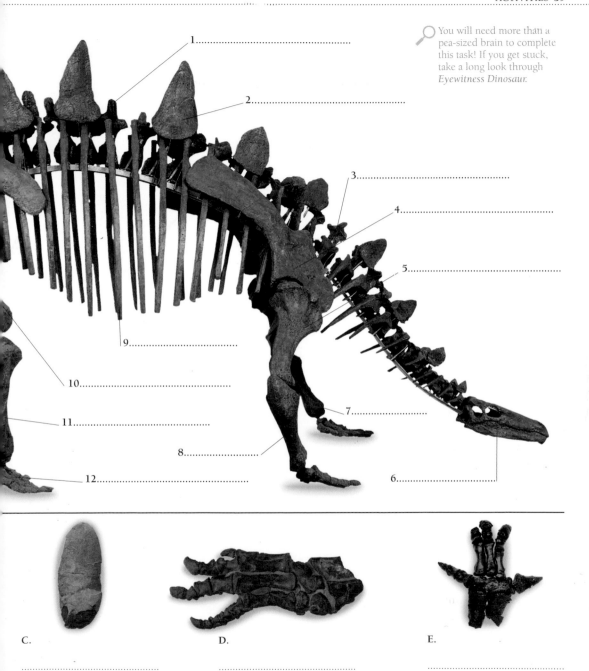

1...

2...

You will need more than a pea-sized brain to complete this task! If you get stuck, take a long look through *Eyewitness Dinosaur*.

3...

4...

5...

9...

10...

11...

8...

12...

7...

6...

C.

....

Dinosaur

....

D.

....

Dinosaur

....

E.

....

Dinosaur

....

EXPERTS' LOG

It's time to get organized and start your own research. Check out the simple tools that every budding expert needs. Your career in paleontology starts here!

At the museum

EXPLORING INDOORS

Tools needed
• Pen
• Notebook
• Camera

• Museum collections give you the chance to see dinosaur fossils and reconstructions close up and find out what dinosaurs looked like, what they ate, and how they evolved.

• Make a note of the information on the display cards. Use the space here, or start your own log in a notebook or scrapbook.

• In addition to housing impressive dinosaur skeletons, many museums have large collections of fossils of other prehistoric animals you might find on your field trips. So you can compare your own finds with those of professional paleontologists!

• Expert guides are often on hand to answer questions. Find out how your favorite dinosaur got its name, where and when it lived, or where its remains have been found.

• If you are going to a region with a substantial fossil site, look for a visitor center or local exhibition displaying finds from that area.

• Many museums allow you to take photographs but not all. If not, visit the souvenir shop where you'll find postcards of your favorite dinosaurs and fossils. Look for models and kits, too.

Natural history museums are the best way to get close to dinosaurs. Some have life-sized reconstructions or real dinosaur bones.

In the field

Although you are unlikely to dig up a dinosaur in your backyard, you can always be on the lookout for fossils of creatures that lived at the same time.

....

....

....

....

....

....

....

....

....

....

Research

TOP TIPS

Books
The first ports of call for any expert are the many reference books available in libraries and bookstores—from comprehensive encyclopedias and visual guides to biographies of your favorite fossil hunters.

The media
Sometimes important finds are made by amateur fossil hunters or in the middle of a construction site or a mine. Keep up to date with the latest reports by taking notes or saving cuttings here or in your scrapbook. Use the *Eyewitness* map in your pack to mark the location of any new finds that you read about.

The web
Search for new dinosaur discoveries online or visit the websites of natural history museums to find details of their latest developments. Check out the websites listed on page 69 of *Eyewitness Dinosaur*.

Museums
Find out about dinosaur collections and temporary exhibitions in your nearest natural history museum. Some may even show you how to analyze your own finds or suggest where you can do more research for yourself.

New dinosaur fossils are being discovered regularly and on every continent, so up-to-date research is an essential part of your study.

....

....

....

....

....

....

....

....

....

Scrapbook

Sketching or photographing any fossils you find in the field or dinosaur exhibits in a museum will help you remember what you've seen. If you can, try drawing how you think the original animals looked, too!

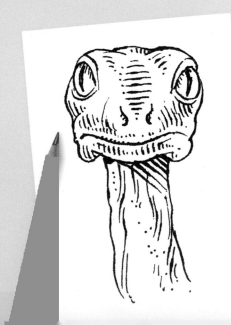

4
PACK MANUAL

Read on for how to get the most out of your interactive expert pack—including step-by-step instructions for making your very own *Tuojiangosaurus*.

Expert reads

Everything you need to know about getting the most from your interactive expert pack is right here! Written by the experts of today for the experts of tomorrow, these reads will speed you on your journey to uncovering the incredible world of dinosaurs. Read on!

Eyewitness Guide

Your first port of call for all things prehistoric, this museum on a page is where you can be an eyewitness to the fascinating lives of dinosaurs. Written by experts and illustrated with fantastic photographs of fossil remains and reconstructions, *Eyewitness Dinosaur* is an essential read for every budding expert.

Wallchart

How were dinosaurs discovered? What were they really like? Put this chart on your wall at home or at school and the answers to your dinosaur questions will never be far away.

OVIRAPTOR
32
OV-ee-RAP-tor "egg thief"

FIELD NOTES
This birdlike di...
It was toothle...
could have c...
was a skele...
mistakenl...

FACT FI...
FAMILY
LENG
Dise
L...
D...

Dinosaur landscape

DINOSAURS LIVED on
world changed substantially during the for nearly 150 million ye
Continents, at first just one great landmass and it is not surprising the
gradually drifted apart until they resembled the
modern arrangement that we are familiar with.
This meant that the climate changed as well, and
both these factors influenced the types of plants
that grew. These changes happened slowly over
millions of years and animals adapted accordingly.
At the beginning of the dinosaur age, low shrubby
fernlike plants dominated the landscape. Then
came a time when huge coiferous forests and
groves of cycads
flourished.
Later on, the
biggest

...ge of all happened when the
...lowering plants began to
...Many plants and flowers
dinosaurs may have
...still be seen
...today.

FIR FEAST
Herbivorous dinosaurs had ample
vegetation to satisfy their appetites.
Duck-billed dinosaurs, such as
Parasaurolophus above, could cope
with tough plants because their jaws
and teeth were so powerful. Even fir
needles posed no problem.

A DINOSAUR HOME
This scene shows
landscape th...
familiar...

CYCAD FRONL
Cycads were abundant
during most of the dinosaur
reign, and are still to be
seen today, although
they are quite rare.

KEY FEATURES
Like reptiles living today, mos
dinosaurs had scaly skin (alth
some had feathers), a long tail,
teeth, and clawed fingers and toe
However, while modern reptiles
walk with their legs sprawled
on each side, dinosaurs walke
upright, with their legs below

Scaly skin

Short, sprawling legs

Sharp claws

Iguana lizard

Early discoveries

In 1820, English doctor Gideon Mantell, who collected
rocks and fossils as a hobby, found some large teeth and
bones. He concluded that they must have belonged to
some kind of giant reptile, which he named *Iguanodon*.

Part of an Iguanodon backbone

Geological timescale

Geologists divide
Earth's history into
time zones, from
its origin around
4,600 million years
ago, to the present
...Dinosaurs

PRECAMBRIAN		4,600–545 million years ago (mya)
	CAMBRIAN PERIOD	545–490 mya
PALAEOZOIC ERA ("ANCIENT LIFE")	ORDOVICIAN PERIOD	490–445 mya
	SILURIAN PERIOD	445–415 mya
	DEVONIAN PERIOD	415–355 mya
	CARBONIFEROUS PERIOD	355–290 mya
	PERMIAN PERIOD	290–250 mya
MESOZOIC ERA MIDDLE LIFE"	TRIASSIC PERIOD	250–200 mya
	JURASSIC PERIOD	200–145 mya
	CRETACEOUS PERIOD	145–65 mya

ALLOSAURUS
al-oh-SAW-rus "different lizard"

FIELD NOTES
One of the most common predators, Allosaur...
plant-eaters throughout the Jurassic world....
head, short neck, a bulky body, and a long...
claws on the ends of its three-fingered arm...
bumps above its eyes.

FACT FILE

FAMILY: Allosauridae	GROUP:
LENGTH: 40 ft (12 m)	WEIG...
DISCOVERED: 1877	BY: Othniel C...
LIVED: 150–145 mya	HABITAT: Plains
DIET: Herbivore	HIP BONE: Lizard hip

42 **THECODONTOSAURUS**
THE-coh-DONT-toe SAW-rus "socket-toothed lizard"

FIELD NOTES
This dinosaur was given its name because of its saw-edged teeth, which were embedded in sockets in the jaw bones. It had a small head and a long tail. Most of the time it walked on two legs, although it could also get around on all fours.

FACT FILE

FAMILY: Anchisauridae	
LENGTH: 7 ft (2.2 m)	GROUP: Prosauropoda
DISCOVERED: 1836	WEIGHT: 110 lb (50 kg)
LIVED: 223–209 mya	BY: Riley & Stutchbury
DIET: Omnivore	HABITAT: Desert plains
	HIP BONE: Lizard hip

Profile Cards

Pull out these handy pocket-size cards and bone up on the essential facts that every expert should know. Use them to test your friends' knowledge, too, or make some of your own cards to add to your collection!

Brow horn

Neck frill

Nose horn

Triceratops skull

DK EYEWITNESS WALL CHARTS

DINOSAUR

DINOSAURS LIVED ON EARTH FOR OVER 150 MILLION YEARS, from 230 million years ago until around 65 million years ago. This extraordinary group of animals ranged in size from gigantic long-necked sauropods to tiny creatures the size of a chicken. Some dinosaurs ate only plants. Others were fierce flesh-eaters. Dinosaurs became extinct long before the first humans. We only know about them because their remains have been preserved in rock as fossils.

Long-necked ske...
This skeleton is of the saur...
When alive, it weighed aro...
(4.2 metric tons) and grew...
(27 m) long. Although the...
has been posed rearing u...
its back legs, scientists ne...
agree that the animal's...
bulk would have...
made this...
impossible.

Pelvis similar to that of birds

Pelvis similar to that of lizards

Gallimimus, a saurischian dinosaur

SLA...
Deino...
eati...
sharp,
claws on...
toes. It proba...
claws into the...
plant-eater, ena...
the animal's bod...
attack on the...
It is though...
encircling...

...osaur hips
...aurs fall into two main groups,
...rding to the structure of their hip bones.
...ithischian ("bird-hipped") dinosaurs were
...plant-eaters. Saurischian ("lizard-hipped")
...osaurs included meat-eaters and the huge,
...nt-eating sauropods.

Hypsilophodon, an ornithischian dinosaur

North America

Europe

Africa

India

South America

Antarctica

Laurasia

Gondwana

TRIASSIC PERIOD
The first dinosaurs appeared during the Triassic Period. At this time, the land was joined together in one huge
...Plants growing

JURASSIC PERIOD
Pangaea slowly split into separate landmasses divided by the ocean. Coniferous forests covered vast areas of land. Plants included ginkgos, monkey puzzle trees, tall tree ferns, and giant horsetails. ...were still no flowering

CRETACEOUS PERIOD
Gondwana and Laurassia broke up into smaller land-masses, beginning the formation of the continents we have today. Flowering plants appeared—the ancestors of today's herbs, flowers, and broad-leaved trees. There were still huge conifer forests, but no grass.

Tails were a u...
for many...

Plotting the past

Paleontologists use a variety of maps to plot different levels of information about dinosaurs. Geological maps indicate the pattern of rock formations in certain areas and the likelihood of fossil finds. Site maps record the position in which dinosaurs bones have been discovered. Geographical maps give a global view of where fossils have been found. Together, these mapping skills help experts piece together a picture of what our planet was like when it was ruled by reptiles.

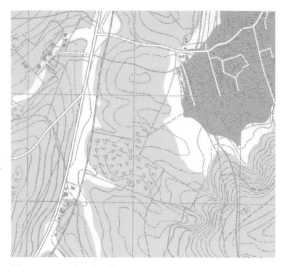

Key to geological map
Upper chalk
Lower chalk
Clay

Geological map
A geological map shows the pattern of rock formations in different areas. Each band of color on this type of map represents a different geological unit—a rock of a certain age—and shows what type of rock is at the surface. Units may be named after the site where they were first described. Fossils usually occur in sedimentary rock, such as chalk, limestone, and sandstone.

Ammonite embedded in seashore rock.

Fossil finds
Hunting for fossils is easiest in places where rocks have become exposed such as beaches, quarries, and the banks of streams. Fossils found loose on the seashore are usually heavier than shells and are uniform in color—generally dark grey or white. Fossils found inland are often embedded within a lump of rock called a nodule, which can be gently eased out of surrounding rocks.

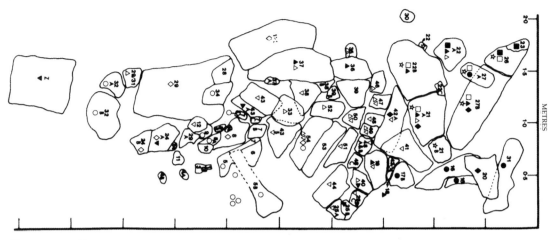

Baryonyx site map

When a fossil hunter unearths a dinosaur skeleton, the position it is found in is carefully recorded. This is a plan of the "crazy paving" of blocks containing *Baryonyx* bones at the brick pit excavation site at Ockley, Surrey, UK. The site was excavated in 1983, and revealed a *Baryonyx* specimen dating back 125 million years.

Distribution map

Although it is impossible to know how many dinosaurs roamed Earth, this *Eyewitness Dinosaur Map* helps us build up a picture of where these incredible creatures lived by plotting the location of fossil findings across the world.

Eyewitness
Dinosaur
Map

The land that time forgot

During the Mesozoic Era (251–65 million years ago), when dinosaurs roamed the Earth, the shape of the land was very different from how it looks a world map today. Dinosaur fossils have been found on every continent, mos recently in Antarctica. Some regions, such as western North America, contain bone-beds crammed with bones of many different dinosaur species, while o areas have yielded only a few bones from a single species. It is impossible to know how many dinosaurs once roamed the Earth, since countless skeleton rotted away before fossilization could occur. Others lie buried still, waiting t be exposed by the elements or excavated by future fossil-hunters.

Multimedia

Handing in school projects has never been so exciting! Packed with specialized images and information about dinosaurs, this clip-art CD will make your homework look so professional you'll be dying to show it off. Go to www.ew.dk.com for more interactive, downloadable information.

Clip-art CD

Parrot head—skull of *Psittacosaurus*.

Preserved insect from millions of years ago.

Ankylosaur nodule

For instant pictures open up your clip-art CD and follow the "how to use" instructions. You'll find the Mesozoic Era at your fingertips!

Footprints and trackways

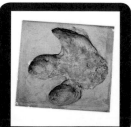

Makeasaurus

Build on your knowledge of dinosaur anatomy
by assembling these pieces of *Tuojiangosaurus*'s body.
You'll find step-by-step instructions on the next page.

Before you start assembling the
dinosaur, press out all the pieces. Match
the numbered slots on each piece with
those on the main frame pieces. Make
sure you push all the slots firmly into
place as you make the model.

Spine and Tail
You must also erect the spine and tail
before you fit the other pieces.
1. Glue spine piece B onto spine piece A,
where it reads: Glue tabs 29 & 30 here.
2. Glue spine piece D onto spine piece C
where it reads: Glue tab 44 here.

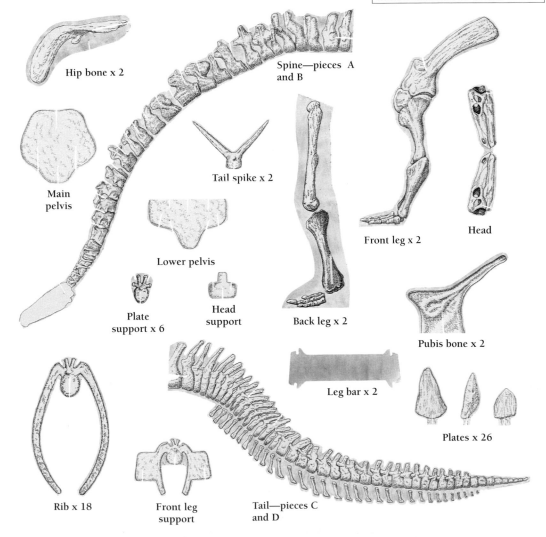

Hip bone x 2

Spine—pieces A
and B

Main
pelvis

Tail spike x 2

Lower pelvis

Plate
support x 6

Head
support

Back leg x 2

Front leg x 2

Head

Pubis bone x 2

Leg bar x 2

Plates x 26

Rib x 18

Front leg
support

Tail—pieces C
and D

1 Slot the two hip bones at right angles into the main pelvis piece, making sure that the folds in the hip bones bend outward and backward.

2 Insert the lower pelvis piece upward into the corresponding slots on each of the hip bones. Check that it is firmly in place.

3 Slot the two pubis bones up into the inner slots of the lower pelvis, making sure they fit on the inside of the hip bones.

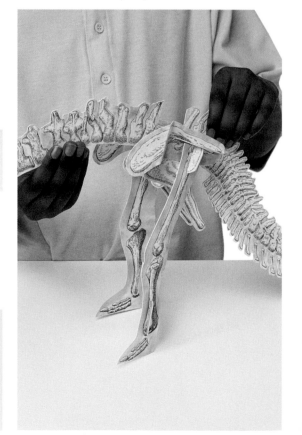

4 Insert the back legs into the outer slots of the lower pelvis. Also connect the legs with the back leg bar, as shown.

5 Connect the main spine piece and the tail piece into the slots on each side of the main pelvis, as shown. Your dinosaur is beginning to take shape!

6 Insert the head support into the top of the spine. Fold both sides of the head back together and insert it into the head support.

7 Take the front leg support (rib 28) and slot both front legs into their corresponding slot numbers. Fold the kneecaps inward along the dotted line.

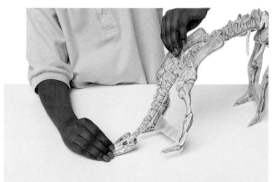

8 Connect the legs with the front leg bar. Now lift the front leg structure over the head and slot the leg support firmly into rib slot 28 of the spine.

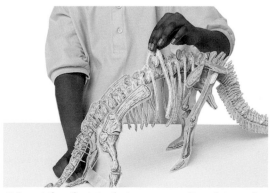

9 Insert the ribs into their corresponding slot numbers all the way down the spine. Push the slots at the top of the front legs into the corresponding slots on rib 32.

10 Insert the small plate supports into the appropriate slots along the entire frame. Make sure they are firmly in place.

11 Finally, slot in the plates up and down the full length of the *Tuojiangosaurus*, as well as the two tail spikes at the end.

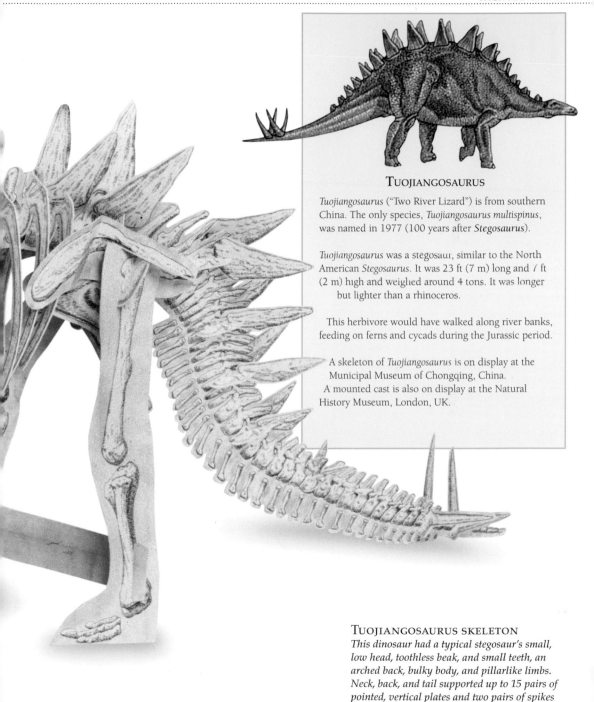

TUOJIANGOSAURUS

Tuojiangosaurus ("Two River Lizard") is from southern China. The only species, *Tuojiangosaurus multispinus*, was named in 1977 (100 years after *Stegosaurus*).

Tuojiangosaurus was a stegosaur, similar to the North American *Stegosaurus*. It was 23 ft (7 m) long and 7 ft (2 m) high and weighed around 4 tons. It was longer but lighter than a rhinoceros.

This herbivore would have walked along river banks, feeding on ferns and cycads during the Jurassic period.

A skeleton of *Tuojiangosaurus* is on display at the Municipal Museum of Chongqing, China. A mounted cast is also on display at the Natural History Museum, London, UK.

TUOJIANGOSAURUS SKELETON
This dinosaur had a typical stegosaur's small, low head, toothless beak, and small teeth, an arched back, bulky body, and pillarlike limbs. Neck, back, and tail supported up to 15 pairs of pointed, vertical plates and two pairs of spikes stuck out from the tip of the tail.

Index

Activity answers

Pages 30–31 Living cousins
Seismosaurus, giraffe, long neck.
Allosaurus, lion, flesh-ripping teeth.
Triceratops, rhinoceros, horned face.
Corythosaurus, duck-billed platypus, wide, flat beak.
Gallimimus, ostrich, fast runner.
Edmontonia, armadillo, armor-plated skin.

Pages 32–33 Who am I?
1. *Anklosaurus*, "fused lizard," plants.
2. *Coelophysis*, "hollow face," meat.
3. *Caudipteryx*, "tail wing," plants.
4. *Seismosaurus*, "earth-shaking lizard," plants.
5. *Plateosaurus*, "flat lizard," both.
6. *Giganotosaurus*, "giant southern lizard," meat.
7. *Eoraptor*, "dawn raptor," meat.
8. *Stegosaurus*, "roof lizard," plants.
9. *Herrerasaurus*, "Hererra's lizard," meat.
10. *Allosaurus*, "different lizard," meat.

Pages 34–35 Dino diets
1. Odd-one-out—omnivore; 2. Meat;
3. Plants; 4. Plants; 5. Plants; 6. Plants;
7. Meat; 8. Meat; 9. Plants.

Botanical quiz
Not around in dinosaur times—wheat, cabbage.

Pages 36–37 Name game
1. *Maiasaura*, "Good mother lizard."
2. *Tyrannosaurus rex*, "King of the tyrant lizards."
3. *Psittacosaurus*, "Parrot lizard."
4. *Protoceratops*, "First-horned face."
5. *Herrerasaurus*, "Herrera's lizard."
6. *Oviraptor*, "Egg thief."

Mixed up
1. *Velociraptor*; 2. *Coelophysis*;
3. *Iguanodon*; 4. *Gallimimus*;
5. *Scelidosaurus*; 6. *Diplodocus*;
7. *Brontosaurus*; 8. *Baryonyx*;
Brontosaurus was renamed *Apatosaurus*.

Pages 38–39 Label it
1. Dorsal vertebra.
2. Cone-shaped plate.
3. Neck bone.
4. Scapula.
5. Humerus.
6. Skull.
7. Radius.
8. Ulna.
9. Rib.
10. Femur.
11. Tibia.
12. Foot metatarsal.
13. Fibula.
14. Pubis.
15. Ischium.
16. Chevron bones.
17. Tail vertebra.
18. Tail spike.
19. Ilium.

This dinosaur is a *Tuojiangosaurus*.

Body parts
A. Hand claw, *Baryonyx*.
B. Tooth, *Edmontosaurus*.
C. Dinosaur eggshell, *Oviraptor*.
D. Foot, *Scelidosaurus*.
E. Hand, *Iguanodon*.

Acknowledgments

The publisher would like to thank the following for their kind permission to reproduce their photographs:

(Key: a–above; b–below/bottom; c–center; l–left; r–right; t–top)

Expert Files
2–3 **Corbis**: Francesc Muntada.
6–7 **Corbis**: Louie Psihoyos.
8–15 courtesy **Luis Chiappe**.
16 **Corbis**: Jonathan Blair (b); Paul A. Souders (t).
7 **Camera Press**: Gamma/Patrick Aventurier). **Corbis**: Richard T. Nowitz (b); Sygma/ard Bisson (t). **DK Images**: Colin Keates
rbis: Michael S. Yamashita (b). Rex s: Peter MacDiarmid (t). Science brary: Mauro Fermariello (c).
s: Louie Psihoyos (r).
Bettmann (t); Louie Psihoyos (b).
Bettmann (r).
Museum of Natural History:

(r). **PA Photos**: AP/Denis Paquin (l).
29 **Corbis**: Louie Psihoyos (b). **Getty Images**: Louie Psihoyos (ca). **Rex Features**: Nils Jorgensen (tr). **Science Photo Library**: Joseph Nettis (cb).
35 **DK Images**: Centaur Studios– modelmakers (cb).
38 **DK Images**: Colin Keates (bl).
40–41 **Corbis**: Louie Psihoyos.
54 **Corbis**: Frank Lane Picture Agency/Derek Hall (b).
55 **The Natural History Museum, London**: (t). **Science Photo Library**: Kenneth W. Fink (b/*Apatosaurus*).

Map
Alamy Images: Wolfgang Kaehler (cr).
Corbis: Richard T. Nowitz (bl); Louie Psihoyos (clb). **Science Photo Library**: Joe Tucciarone (crb).

Profile
See page 16 of *Dinosaur Profile Cards*

Wall chart
See page 72 of *Eyewitness Dinosaur*

Clip-art CD
See the *Credits* file on the CD

All other images © Dorling Kindersley
For further information see:
www.dkimages.com

The publisher would also like to thank:
Ed Merritt for cartography on the Eyewitness Map;
Lynn Bresler for proofreading & the index;
Neil Lockley & Lisa Stock for editorial assistance.
Margaret Parrish for Americanization.